LIVEWIRE
REAL LIVES

Tom Cruise

Julia Holt

Published in association with The Basic Skills Agency

Hodder & Stoughton

A MEMBER OF THE HODDER HEADLINE GROUP

Acknowledgements

*Photos: The Ronald Grant Archive supplied the following: pp. 3, 19 © Universal. p. 6 © 1981 Twentieth
Century-Fox Film Corp, pp. 10, 13 and 19
The Kobal Collection supplied p. 16 © Touchstone 1986.
p. 21 © London Features International Ltd.*
Cover photo: © London Features.

Orders: please contact Bookpoint Ltd, 39 Milton Park, Abingdon, Oxon OX14 4TD. Telephone:
(44) 01235 400414, Fax: (44) 01235 400454. Lines are open from 9.00–6.00, Monday to Saturday,
with a 24 hour message answering service. Email address: orders@bookpoint.co.uk

British Library Cataloguing in Publication Data
Holt, Julia
   Tom Cruise. – (Real lives) (Livewire)
   1. Cruise, Tom. – Juvenile literature   2. Motion picture actors
   and actresses — United States — Biography — Juvenile
   literature   3. Readers
   I. Title   II. Wilson, Mike
   791.4'3'028'092

ISBN 0 340 701129

First published 1997
Impression number 10 9 8 7 6 5 4 3 2
Year 2004 2003 2002 2001 2000 1999 1998

Typeset by Fakenham Photosetting Ltd, Fakenham, Norfolk.
Printed in Great Britain for Hodder & Stoughton Educational, a division of Hodder Headline Plc,
338 Euston Road, London NW1 3BH by Page Bros, Norwich.

Contents

Beginning

Only two men in his family
have lived past the age of 50.
Maybe that's why Tom Cruise
puts more effort
into living every day
than most people do.

He is dyslexic.
He comes from a broken home.
But he is now
the most successful film star in the world.

Men want to be like him
and women want to be with him.

He has a happy family life
and Hollywood at his feet.
But life has not always been so good
to Tom Cruise.

His father had a <u>dream</u> of being <u>rich</u>.
So the family moved house
to <u>chase</u> that dream.

Tom was born in 1962.
In his first eleven years
the family moved house seven times.
He also had to move schools.
This made learning difficult.

So did his dyslexia.
The words on the page
moved as he read.
He mixed up *b*s and *d*s.
His teachers said he was stupid
but his mother knew he wasn't.
It was a difficulty
that she and his sisters had.

Even today
he has a dictionary with him
to check spellings.

Tom has always had difficulty reading. He suffers from dyslexia.

Tom made up
for his difficulties at school
by being very good at sport.

When he was 12,
his parents split up.
Tom became the man in his family.
His father didn't send money
and they didn't see him again
for ten years.

Tom enjoyed the company
of his mother and three sisters.
Today he prefers
the company of women.
He says,
'I've always had women
as my best friends.
I trust women.'

In his last year at school,
he hurt his knee
and couldn't play sports.
What he did next
changed his life.

He took part in a school play
and he loved it.

At 17 when the other kids
left home for college,
Tom went to New York
to be an actor.
He said,
'I felt I needed to act.'

He gave <u>himself</u>
ten years to make it.
Success, when it came,
was much faster than that.

Tom had a leading part in his first film, *Taps*.

First films

At first
he had to get used
to being turned down.
He got a job as a handy man
to make a living.
He was 19
and nothing was going to get in his way.

His big break came
with a small part
in the film *Taps*.
Two thousand other men
wanted a part in that film.

As soon as they started filming
they saw how good Tom was.
They gave him a lead part.

Taps has an anti-military story
and it wasn't a hit at the time.
But Tom Cruise
was being talked about
in Hollywood.

He was called
a star of the 'Brat Pack'.
They were a bunch of young actors
who seemed to be
in every top film.
Tom didn't like this.
He didn't want to be one of a bunch.
He wanted to stand out.

His next film was called *Losin' It*.
This one was a mistake.
One critic said the story was
'Kids get drunk.
Kids get laid.
Kids go home.'

Tom needed a better agent.
He needed to be more choosy
about his films.

Tom Cruise is a method actor.
This means
he does everything he can
to feel the same
as the person he's playing.

For his next film,
he didn't wash for weeks.
He played the part
of a greaser in *The Outsiders*.

It's a film about
two rival gangs of kids.
It was made in 1983.
It was a hit at the time
and it's now a classic.
People still watch it on video.

They grew up on the outside of society.
They weren't looking for a fight.
They were looking to belong.

FRANCIS FORD COPPOLA
PRESENTS

The
Outsiders

S. E. Hinton's classic novel
about youth.

Can you spot Patrick Swayze, Matt Dillon, Rob Lowe and
Tom Cruise?

In the same year,
Tom also made a comedy called
Risky Business.
In the film he plays a boy
who has rich parents.
His parents go away for the weekend.
He meets a call girl.
Together,
they turn his parents' house into a brothel.
He dances around the house
in only socks and underpants.

Tom wanted to do more serious films.
He didn't want to play
a boy all his life.

Just before his next film,
his long-lost father
came home to die.
Tom went to see him,
but he didn't find out
where his father had been.
His father died without telling him.

Action

After the funeral,
Tom flew to London.
He started work on *Legend*.
It was a slow and difficult film to make.

Thirty seconds of film
could take a week to make.
Then a fire burned down the set.

When the fairy story film
was finally made,
it was beautiful.
But not successful.

Tom didn't want to do
that kind of film again.
He wanted to do
an action film.

Top Gun
was just the film he wanted to make.
He even helped
to write the story.

Tom in *Top Gun*.

Top Gun is a film
about life in a flying school
for fighter pilots.

Before he started work
he spent three months
with fighter pilots.
He got to know the people
and their way of life.

It was the biggest film of 1986.
It made $170 million in the USA.
But critics said
that Tom was too nice for the part.

This upset Tom.
On top of this, he was lonely.
Over the last six years
he had dated many women.
Some of them famous,
like Cher.
He was rich,
but he had no-one to share it with.

First love

Back in 1961
Paul Newman made a film
about a pool player, called *The Hustler*.
Twenty-five years later
he wanted to play the part again.
This time Tom was a young hustler
and Paul Newman the older, wiser player.

The film was called
The Color of Money
and it was made in 49 days.
Tom was proud
of his part in this film.

Paul Newman
became a father figure to him.
He showed Tom how to race cars.

Tom took his new girlfriend, Mimi,
car racing.
They fell in love
and were married in 1987.

Tom and Paul Newman in *The Color of Money*.

Mimi was a member
of the Church of Scientology.
Soon Tom became a member.
He says
'Scientology has helped me
to become more me.'

Tom and Mimi wanted children,
but it didn't happen.

They went to Jamaica
where Tom made the film *Cocktail*.

Some said
the film was flashy
and shallow.
Critics said that
it was the worst film of the year.
The public didn't think so.
Cocktail made a lot of money
and Tom was now waiting
to make *Rain Man*.

Blockbuster

In *Rain Man*
Tom played a smooth car salesman.
Dustin Hoffman played his brother,
a man with learning difficulties.
Tom's dyslexia helped him to understand
this man's difficulties.

The film did not have
a happy ending.
People said it would not be popular.
But it won eight Oscars.
It was a blockbuster.

In 1988
Tom made another anti-military film.
It was called
Born on the Fourth of July.
It was the true story
of a Vietnam veteran
who came home in a wheelchair.

It had a hard-hitting story.
It said,
war is a waste of life.
In this film
Tom proved he could act.

Tom in *Born on the Fourth of July*.

New love

He met Nicole Kidman
when they made
a car racing film together.

As soon as he met Nic
he knew his three-year marriage
was over.

Tom divorced Mimi
and married Nic in 1990.
He gave her a big diamond ring
and a red sports car.
They became
the best-known couple in Hollywood.

Tom and Nic spent 1991
making a film together.
It was called *Far and Away*.
The film didn't make much money.
It only made $100 million.
That's not a success for Tom Cruise.

Tom with his wife, Nicole Kidman.

In his next film he played a lawyer.
It was called *A Few Good Men*.
Jack Nicholson
nearly acted better than Tom.
He nearly stole the show.
But Tom acted well too
and stopped him.

Tom played a lawyer again
in *The Firm*.

He felt he was getting sidetracked,
playing the same part again and again.
He needed something
to get his teeth into.
That film was on its way.

Tom wanted a baby
more than he wanted an Oscar.
In January 1993,
he and Nic adopted a baby girl.
They called her Isabella.
She turned their lives
upside down.

Tom had never played a villain before.
In *Interview with a Vampire*
he got the chance.
Lestat the vampire is a mass murderer.
He sinks his teeth
into every man, woman and child
he meets.

A lot of people
said Tom couldn't play the vampire.
They said,
'he's too nice.'

It was a difficult film to make.
When it came out it made money
and Tom was happy with it.
But some critics said
Brad Pitt was better than him.

Back home in LA
Tom had the idea of making
Mission: Impossible.
Thirty years ago it was a TV show.

By the end of 1994
they started work.

Film and family

In the middle of making the film
Tom and Nic adopted a baby boy.
His name was Connor.

All the family went to Prague
to watch Tom
play the spy Ethan Hunt.
Then they all went to London
for five months
to finish the film.

Mission: Impossible
cost $64 million to make.
It had two big stunts.
Tom did them both himself.

He hung on top of a speeding train.
He got out of the way
of a 30 foot wall of water.
Connor slept
while all of this went on.

This action film
was loved by film goers.
The critics said
it was all about two stunts.

Tom in *Mission: Impossible*.

Tom Cruise still has Hollywood
at his feet.

He played a hero in real life
in August 1996.
Tom and his family
were on their yacht
off the coast of Italy.
They saw another yacht on fire
and they saved five people
and no-one was hurt.

In 1996,
Jerry Maguire hit the cinemas
in America.

Tom plays Jerry Maguire,
a ruthless sports agent.
He gets the sack
and has to stake everything
on one American football player.
Jerry has to make him
a success.

The film was a success
in the US.
It made $102 million
in its first six weeks.

Tom said
he did not want
to be in another film with Nic.

But he is,
and it's called
Eyes Wide Shut.
It was made
on a closed set.
They kept it a big secret.

Maybe this time
Tom and Nic
will have success together.

Mission: Impossible 2
will be with us
in 1998,
and Tom Cruise
will play Ethan Hunt again.

It's no surprise
that Tom Cruise
says his life is magic
with Nic, the kids and his work.